home spa

Stephanie Donaldson

home spa

top-to-toe beauty treatments for total well-being

LORENZ BOOKS

This edition is published by Lorenz Books
Lorenz Books is an imprint of Anness Publishing Limited
Hermes House, 88–89 Blackfriars Road, London SE1 8HA

© Anness Publishing Limited 2002

Published in the USA by Lorenz Books, Anness Publishing Inc
27 West 20th Street, New York, NY 10011; fax 212 807 6813

Published in Australia by Lorenz Books, Anness Publishing Pty Ltd
tel. 02 89208622; fax 02 8920 8633

This edition distributed in the UK by Aurum Press Ltd
tel 020 7637 3225; fax 020 7580 2469

This edition distributed in the USA by National Book Network
tel 301 459 3366; fax 301 459 1705; www.nbnbooks.com

This edition distributed in Canada by General Publishing
tel 416 445 3333; fax 416 445 5991; www.genpub.com

This edition distributed in New Zealand by David Bateman Ltd
tel 09 415 7664; fax 09 415 8892

A CIP catalogue record for this book is available from the
British Library

Publisher JOANNA LORENZ
Managing editor JUDITH SIMONS
Senior art manager CLARE REYNOLDS
Project editor SARAH AINLEY
Copy editors GILLY CAMERON COOPER AND RAJE AIREY
Editorial reader RICHARD MCGINLAY
Indexer HELEN SNAITH
Designers OPTA DESIGN AND MARK LATTER
Photography MICHELLE GARRETT
Additional photography DEBBIE PATTERSON
Production controller CLAIRE RAE

1 3 5 7 9 10 8 6 4 2

Note to reader
The suggestions in this book are not intended as a substitute for
serious medical or psychotic conditions. Please seek a medical
opinion if you have doubts about your health. Neither the author
nor the publisher can accept liability for failure to follow this advice.

contents

first steps to...

Going to a spa has never been easier. Turn your home into a
haven for health and well-being and follow this unique three-step
programme for a fitter, healthier, more radiant you – step one:
detox, refresh, revive; step two: relax, let go, balance; step three:
restore, strengthen, heal. Work through the programme for
a complete overhaul of body and mind, or dip in for shorter,
quick-fix treatments. Whichever you decide, the following pages
contain a wealth of treatment tips, recipes and information,
all geared to suit your mood and personal needs.

...a new you

spas ancient and modern

Civilizations throughout the world have valued the healing powers of water. To the ancient Greeks, it was the elixir of life, and temples to the god of medicine were built near hot springs. The word "spa" means a curative mineral spring and is derived from the town of Spa in Belgium. The practice of "taking the waters" became popular in Roman times, when people enjoyed water treatments followed by massage with fragrant oils and lotions.

Today it is possible to enjoy spa treatments at home, maximizing the benefits by combining water treatments with diet, exercise and natural therapies. So enjoy a little pampering and book some spa dates in your diary, tailoring the programme to your needs. Spa treatments have countless benefits for body, mind and soul, whether it's to detox and revive, relax and unwind, or restore and heal – the choice is yours.

TOP Gather together in advance whatever materials or pieces of equipment you will need for treatments such as this essential oil compress.

LEFT Spa time is not to be rushed. You need to be in a receptive state beforehand, and allow for recovery time; creating a soothing enviroment will help you achieve this.

OPPOSITE To make the whole experience more pleasurable, choose decorative bottles and dishes for home-blended essential oils, creams and lotions.

environment and mood

The Romans recognized the sensual and therapeutic power of fragrance. The emperor Nero relaxed in warm baths scented with rosemary and bay. You too can create a sensual haven, soothing away everyday concerns in a warm and fragrant atmosphere.

To create your sanctuary, use candles to give out a subtle, flickering light. Scented candles are available, or else vaporize essential oils in a burner. Include fresh flowers and houseplants to add a sense of luxury and natural beauty. Have available a good supply of freshly laundered thick, warm towels and a loose-fitting bathrobe. Towelling ones are best for spa treatments as they absorb moisture.

Get to know the different properties of herbs and oils and use them to suit your different moods and needs. There is a scent, a soap and a lotion for every occasion. Assemble your ingredients with thought and care, adding your favourite reading materials or music, and you are ready to switch off from the world outside and begin your home spa treatment.

treatments and therapies

Spa treatments were originally based on water. Water is essential to life and our bodies are largely composed of this element. Taking a shower, enjoying a lazy bath, using steam inhalations to clear blocked pores and open the sinuses, plus drinking plenty of water and eating food with a high water content (raw fruits and vegetables) can all form part of your home spa session. Add to this the therapeutic use of herbs

and essential oils, pampering your body with naturally fragranced shampoos, soaps, creams and lotions, enjoying the health-giving benefits of herbal drinks plus using natural healing remedies to trigger a self-healing process, and you will soon notice the positive effect on how you look and feel.

Remember too that exercise and deep relaxation also have important parts to play in your spa regime. Together, they will tone and strengthen your body, refresh and rejuvenate your soul, and help you to cope with the stresses and strains of modern life.

There are many different types of therapy that you can use in your home spa. The following is an overview of the treatments used in this book:

Hydrotherapy is the official term for water therapies. These include the therapeutic use of water (hot and cold) in baths, showers and steam inhalations to improve the circulation, cleanse and refresh the body, and to aid relaxation. Sweating, whether through hot steam inhalations, or through exercise, plays an important role in spa treatments as many toxins are released through the skin.

Aromatherapy is the therapeutic use of fragrance using essential plant oils. Each oil has particular healing properties, with the power to affect the mind, body and emotions. The oils can be used in a variety of ways. They may be used in the shower or in the bath, or added to creams, lotions and massage "base" oils (such as almond oil) and rubbed into the body. You can also vaporize the oils in an aromatherapy oil-burner or steam inhalation and breathe deeply on the healing fragrance. Select the oils that most closely match your needs.

Herbalism is the use of plants for health and well-being. Herbal preparations are made using a plant's fresh or dried leaves, stems, flowers, roots or other plant parts. These may then be used in herbal teas, in beauty products or in steam inhalations, for instance. Herbal remedies are also available commercially in capsule form.

Bach flower essences are very useful for treating negative mental and emotional states. The remedies are made from infusions of the flower-heads of particular plants and trees, preserved in alcohol. The remedies are best taken in a glass of water or under the tongue, 2–3 drops at a time.

OPPOSITE A few drops of an essential oil on a tissue can be sniffed for immediate relief, or placed inside your shirt so that you benefit from the aroma throughout the day.

TOP A steam inhalation can be used to relieve head colds and sinus congestion, or as a skin treatment to open up blocked pores.

RIGHT Home-made remedies made from fresh aromatic herbs are a satisfying way to bring relief from common everyday problems such as tension headaches.

ABOVE Complement your spa programme with herb or spice teas and tisanes – different ingredients can boost energy, help you relax, or cleanse your system.

OPPOSITE Using an oil burner is a popular way of vaporizing essential oils. You may need to keep adding to the water in the top to stop it drying out.

14 first steps to a new you

Homeopathy uses natural plant or mineral substances that are diluted many times over. The remedies are taken internally in the form of a tasteless pill. They work on the whole person, stimulating the body to heal itself and can be safely used to treat acute conditions, such as a hangover headache, muscle and joint pain, or coughs and colds. Homeopathy will not work if taken in conjunction with peppermint or eucalyptus, which cancel out homeopathic action.

Massage uses the power of touch to bring comfort and healing. It stimulates the circulation, eases out muscular tension and encourages the release of toxins. Depending on the strokes used, massage can be stimulating or relaxing and encourages the body's self-healing process. It promotes feelings of calm and well-being and is good for stress and anxiety.

Reflexology applies thumb or finger pressure to mapped-out points on the soles of the feet. These points are linked to the rest of the body by invisible energy channels, and by working the feet, the health benefits are felt throughout the body. It is a very relaxing therapy.

Yoga has, in recent years, become extremely popular as a therapeutic technique. It involves easing the body into different postures to increase flexibility in the joints, stretch and strengthen the muscles and release nervous and physical tension. It is a form of gentle exercise that encourages relaxation and restores balance and harmony in body and mind.

Meditation is to sit and do nothing, closing your eyes and drawing your attention away from the outside world, letting your thoughts come and go as they please. Meditation nourishes your inner self. It is refreshing and relaxing, helping to soothe and rebalance body and mind, and can be as beneficial as a good night's sleep.

Nutrition therapy is based on the role of diet in health and well-being. If we are making poor dietary choices, our health will suffer. We can improve our health and vitality with healing and cleansing foods and by reducing our intake of foods that place a strain on the body's resources. Vitamin and mineral supplements may be taken to address dietary deficiencies.

detox — refresh — revive

Herbs and essential oils: cedarwood, lemon, geranium, cypress, juniper, lavender, valerian, marjoram, neroli, rose otto, bergamot, frankincense

Bach flowers: crab apple (detoxifier), hornbeam (clarity, enthusiasm), gentian (cheerfulness and optimism)

relax — let go — balance

Herbs and essential oils: lavender, chamomile, valerian, hops, marjoram, melissa, geranium, borage, St John's wort, ylang ylang

Bach flowers: white chestnut (inability to relax, mind won't switch off), vervain (stress and tension), impatiens (irritability)

restore — strengthen — heal

Herbs and essential oils: lavender, tea tree, garlic, eucalyptus, marigold, evening primrose, echinacea, sage, rose, neroli, geranium, myrrh

Bach flowers: olive (complete exhaustion), walnut (protection from negative influences)

safety notes

• All the ingredients mentioned in this book have been chosen with safety in mind. Always carefully follow the directions for quantities, method and storage. If you have sensitive skin, test skin products on a small patch on the inside of the wrist or elbow before using.

• If you are pregnant, or suffer from an existing medical condition, or if you are in any doubt about whether a treatment is right for you, consult your doctor or a professional practitioner who is qualified in the relevant field.

• Take care when using essential oils. These are highly concentrated, medicinal substances and, with few exceptions, should not be applied neat on to the skin.

• Always replace the caps of essential oil bottles and put the bottles away after use. Store them in a cool, dark place, out of the reach of children and pets.

• Do not use essential oils near the eyes and do not take them internally (organic essential oils may be used in mouthwashes and gargles). Citrus oils, especially bergamot, are light-sensitive, so do not use on the skin before exposure to sunlight.

detox
refresh
revive

Our bodies are exposed to a constant bombardment of toxins from pollution, smoke, and unhealthy food and additives. It's time to have a deep, deep clean, to revitalize body and mind, and leave you feeling fresh and ready to start again.

preparing to detox

Many common ailments are related to a build-up of toxins in the body. Painful joints, skin problems, excess mucus, headaches and a weakened immune system may all be signs that the body is not coping with the amount of poisons in the system. Persistent tiredness, low energy, feeling emotionally "down", mental confusion and fogginess, are also indicators that the body is overloaded and not able to function properly. It is like living in a house full of junk!

What is needed is a thorough cleanse, followed by healthier lifestyle habits to help your system stay clean and fresh. A sedentary lifestyle, alcohol, caffeine and sugar, plus the chemical residues found in foodstuffs, all place a strain on the body's resources. Drink at least six large glasses of water a day to flush out the body, and substitute tea and coffee with herbal teas. Eat fresh fruit and raw or lightly cooked vegetables, and take regular exercise. The Bach flower remedy crab apple is a useful detoxifier. Add 3–4 drops to a glass of water and sip slowly.

TOP Eat a varied selection of fresh fruit every day, choosing pesticide-free organic produce if possible.

LEFT Eating plenty of fresh raw vegetables and salads will supply valuable minerals and vitamins, and will help to keep your energy levels high.

mint tea

Mint tea is a deliciously refreshing drink, served in many hot countries as a reviver. It also helps the digestive system to work more effectively. Avoid drinking it at bedtime, as it may keep you awake.

250ml/8fl oz/1 cup water
1–2 sprigs fresh mint/5ml/1 tsp dried mint
honey (optional)

Fill a non-aluminium pan with the water and bring to the boil. Turn off the heat and add the mint. Cover and leave to infuse (steep) for 5–10 minutes. Strain off the liquid and drink. Add a little honey to sweeten, if you like.

deep-cleansing facials

A glowing complexion is a fantastic beauty asset and a sign of good health. Our facial skin is delicate and needs regular cleansing to keep the pores dirt free so that the skin can breathe. A facial scrub will remove the dead skin cells and stimulate the circulation, bringing fresh oxygenated blood to the surface, and leaving the skin clean and soft.

Scrubs are usually made with a "gritty" ingredient, such as oatmeal. For a once-a-week facial scrub, combine 45ml/3 tbsp each of ground skinned almonds, medium oatmeal and powdered milk with 30ml/2 tbsp of powdered rose petals. Store in a sealed glass jar.

To use it, take a handful and mix to a soft paste with a little almond oil. Apply gently in a circular motion, avoiding the delicate skin around the eyes and mouth. Leave for 10 minutes and wash off with warm water.

steams and masks

A facial steam sauna will open the pores, helping to remove impurities. Pour boiling water into a bowl and sit in front of it, making a tent around your head and shoulders with a towel. Keep your face 30cm/12in above the steam, for as long as is comfortable. Repeat two or three times. For added benefit, stir herbs or essential oils into the water: chamomile (dry skin), rosemary (oily skin) and lavender (normal skin) are all suitable. Use 40g/1$^{1}/_{2}$oz fresh/15g/$^{1}/_{2}$oz dried herbs or 2 drops essential oil to 600ml/1 pint/2$^{1}/_{2}$ cups water.

After you have opened the pores, the deep-cleansing action of a face mask will be more effective. The mask will also tighten the skin. Herbal masks should be used every two weeks (every three weeks if your skin is dry): any more and they can be over-stimulating.

Caution: Do not use a facial sauna if you have a tendency to thread veins or if you are asthmatic.

LEFT Fresh chamomile can be added to a facial sauna.

for oily skin

parsley and sage mask

15g/¹/₂oz fresh parsley and sage, mixed together

300ml/¹/₂ pint/1¹/₄ cups boiling water

30ml/2 tbsp fine oatmeal

15ml/1 tbsp Fuller's earth

1 egg white

5ml/1 tsp lemon juice

for dry skin

comfrey and rose water mask

6 comfrey leaves

150ml/¹/₄ pint/²/₃ cup boiling water

30ml/2 tbsp fine oatmeal

1 egg yolk

5ml/1 tsp honey

5ml/1 tsp rose water

a little milk or natural (plain) yogurt to mix

To use either mask, mix together the ingredients to make a smooth, thick paste and apply evenly over the face and neck, avoiding the sensitive eye and mouth areas. Lie back, close your eyes and relax for 15–20 minutes as the mask dries and tightens up the skin. Rinse off with tepid water and pat the skin dry.

Masks, scrubs and steams draw out moisture as well as grime. After any deep-cleansing treatment, remember to use plenty of moisturizer – make two applications – using a product suitable for your skin type.

eye and face refreshers

Tiredness, toxic overload, mental stress, anxieties and emotional problems can make our eyes look dull and lifeless, and give our complexion an unhealthy pallor. Treat yourself with these reviving spa tonics to tone the skin and refresh tired eyes.

The skin around the eyes is the most delicate on the face and the first to show signs of weariness or stress. The most effective eye-revival package combines simple treatment with gentle moisturizing and rest. Place cucumber slices or an ordinary used teabag (cooled and squeezed) over your eyes and lie back and rest for 10–15 minutes. The tannin in the teabag is a mild astringent and will firm the skin, while cucumber is cooling and refreshing. Afterwards, pat the skin dry and moisturize using a gentle eye cream.

skin tonics

Use a skin tonic after deep-cleansing to leave your skin feeling fresh and invigorated. Tonics are especially useful if you live in a hard-water area, as lime scale deposits in the water can disrupt the skin's delicate pH balance, causing dryness and irritation. Home-prepared skin tonics are easy to make, using a mixture of either floral water or cider vinegar, together with herbs or essential oils. They must be kept chilled after making and used within a few days if you are using herbs, or a few weeks if you are using essential oils.

LEFT It is important to moisturize the skin around the eyes after an eye-revival session. Wait a few minutes after the treatment to allow the skin to rest, then apply your favourite moisturizing cream to the whole of the area.

summer rose toner

40g/1¹/₂oz fresh rose petals

600ml/1 pint/2¹/₂ cups boiling water

15ml/1 tbsp cider vinegar

Put the rose petals in a heatproof bowl and pour
over the boiling water. Add the cider vinegar, cover
and leave to stand for 2 hours. Strain the liquid
into a clean screw-topped bottle.

for oily skin
lavender tonic

25g/1oz dried lavender flowers

475ml/16fl oz/2 cups boiling water

25ml/1¹/₂tbsp witch hazel

Infuse (steep) the lavender in the water for
20–30 minutes. Strain the cooled liquid into
a screw-topped jar and add the witch hazel.

adapt for your skin type
essential oil tonics

90ml/6 tbsp rose water or orange flower water

5ml/1 tsp cider vinegar

4–6 drops essential oil for your skin type

Put the water and vinegar in a screw-topped bottle
and add the chosen oils depending on your skin type:
chamomile, lavender, neroli (dry/sensitive); bergamot,
frankincense, cypress (oily), geranium, lavender,
rose otto (normal). Close the bottle and shake well
to disperse the oils, and leave to stand overnight.

body focus

Take care of your body and you will enjoy greater benefit from your home spa treatments. Regular body care makes it easier for your system to detox, and this will make your body more receptive to the therapeutic effects of revitalizing nutrients and oils in your everyday diet and in the treatments and therapies you use as part of your spa programme.

exercise and diet

Make regular exercise and a healthy eating plan part of your home spa treatment routine. Walking, swimming, cycling, working out and yoga are all great ways to stay fit, increase your stamina and keep your body toned and supple. Try to give yourself at least three twenty-minute exercise sessions a week.

Exercise boosts the circulation, allowing the body to absorb nutrients and eliminate toxins and waste more efficiently. It also helps combat and deal with cellulite. Cellulite gives areas of the skin a lumpy, orange-peel effect, believed to be caused by waste materials and toxins building up in the body tissues to create pockets of water, fat and impurities. Cutting down on sugary foods, drinking plenty of water and eating more fresh fruit and raw vegetables will also help the body to deal with cellulite.

ABOVE A scrub made from ground almonds, rose petals, oatmeal and orange peel is a gentle alternative to a loofah.

OPPOSITE TOP After an exfoliating body scrub and a warm shower, dry yourself, then apply a moisturizing emulsion to the skin, using gentle circular movements.

OPPOSITE BELOW Vigorous massage can help to disperse cellulite by improving lymphatic drainage.

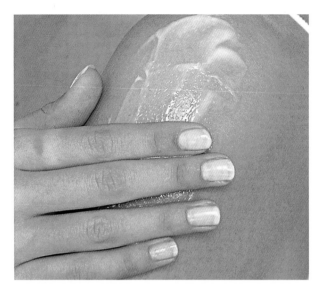

body skin care

The skin is the body's largest organ and forms a protective barrier against bacteria and other invaders. Although it continually sheds and renews itself, the skin has a lot to cope with, and it deserves special attention. Body scrubs remove dead skin cells and stimulate the blood supply to the skin, leaving it tingling and toned.

This scrub makes a delightful alternative to a loofah. It is also gentle on the skin and pleasantly aromatic. Mix 45ml/3 tbsp each of ground sunflower seeds, medium oatmeal, flaked sea salt and finely grated orange peel with 3 drops of grapefruit essential oil. This reviving scrub can be used once a week. If stored in a sealed glass jar it will keep for several

months. To use, mix as much as you need with almond oil to make a thick paste, then rub over the whole body, paying particular attention to areas of dry skin such as the elbows and knees. Wipe off any residue with tissues before showering or bathing.

detoxifying massage

Body massages are generally restorative and healing, but here is one with particular cleansing qualities. Add 1 drop of fennel and 2 drops juniper essential oil to 15ml/1 tbsp almond oil. Rub the oil into your skin with your fingertips, using a circular movement. Better still, lie down on a towel and ask someone to do it for you! Both fennel and juniper oils have detoxifying, purifying properties. Focus on any areas of cellulite; it should help.

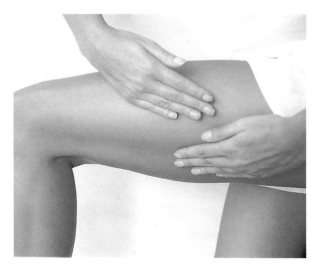

clean healthy hair

Hair moves better when it is clean and healthy. Its colour and texture are fixed by genetics, but the strength and condition are governed by how you treat it, your diet and state of mind. If you are stressed or tired, your hair will look dull and lifeless. Vitamin B complex supplements or foods such as liver, wholegrain cereals and brewer's yeast can help to boost hair condition. Vitamin C is important for strong, healthy capillaries that supply blood to the hair follicles, while evening primrose oil can improve the appearance of skin and hair.

aromatic shampoos

For beautiful, fresh-smelling hair, it is worth making your own shampoos. Add 4–6 drops of essential oil to 60ml/4 tbsp of an unfragranced shampoo. Choose from the following oils: chamomile, geranium, lavender (normal hair); ylang ylang, rosemary (dry hair); juniper, tea tree (for dandruff or scalp problems); or eucalyptus and citrus oils (greasy, lank hair).

TOP Mix 15ml/1 tbsp of dried or fresh herbs, such as chamomile, into 60ml/4 tbsp of an unperfumed shampoo base for your own personalized hair treatment.

LEFT Wholegrain cereals, such as bread, are an excellent source of B vitamins, which keep hair strong and healthy.

hair wash

As a general rule, the less often you wash your hair
the better. Frequent washing removes the natural
oils from the scalp so try to avoid over-washing –
if your style needs a boost, just dampen the
hair slightly to revive whatever treatments
are already in it. Before you wash your
hair, brush out loose hairs and dirt
with a soft brush. Wash in
lukewarm water, gently
massaging in the shampoo
with the fingertips in
a circular motion.
Rinse thoroughly.

mouth fresheners

Give your mouth a special treat with home-made herbal preparations. These are far gentler than commercial antiseptic mouthwashes, which can upset the natural acid balance of the mouth.

A pleasant tasting mouthwash is made with 5ml/ 1 tsp each of ground nutmeg, cloves, cardamom pods and caraway seeds, and a handful of fresh lemon verbena leaves (or 15g/^{1}/$_2$oz dried). Put the spices and lemon verbena in a pan with 600ml/1 pint/2^1/$_2$ cups water, and simmer for 30 minutes. Strain through a sieve lined with kitchen paper, then pour into bottle. To use, dilute 15–30ml/1–2 tbsp in a glass of water.

Clean teeth fight off harmful bacteria and plaque and will keep your breath fresh. For strong teeth, include plenty of calcium in your diet from dairy products and fresh green vegetables, and vitamin D from oily fish, eggs and dairy produce. Eat avocados, bananas, meat and potatoes for potassium, and pulses (legumes), nuts and cereals for magnesium.

TOP Garden herbs can contribute to your mouth detox: chewing parsley can help dispel garlic-drenched breath.

LEFT Fresh sage leaves (25g/1oz) can be chopped and mixed with 60ml/4 tsp of sea salt ,and baked in a low oven for 1 hour until crisp. Pound to a fine powder, then sprinkle on to a damp toothbrush to use.

lavender mouthwash

15ml/1 tbsp dried lavender

300ml/$^1/_2$ pint/$1^1/_4$ cups mineral water

30ml/2 tbsp sweet sherry

Add the lavender to a pan containing the mineral water
and simmer for 30 minutes. Strain through a sieve
lined with kitchen paper and add the sweet sherry.
Pour the mix into a clean screw-topped bottle and
store in a cool dark place. The alcohol acts as a
preservative, so the mix will keep for up to 1 month.
To use, dilute 15–30ml/1–2 tbsp in a glass of water
and gargle at the back of the mouth.

shower revivers

No home spa treatment is complete without a shower. If you can stand it, a tepid or cold shower is refreshing and energizing. If you can't, add 2–3 drops of essential oil to your sponge and rub it briskly all over your body under warm running water. Rosemary, peppermint or basil are classic refreshers, while grapefruit blended with geranium makes a detoxifying, stimulating mix.

BELOW A dusting powder is a wonderful way to coat the body with fragrance. If you customize a powder by adding an essential oil, the effect will be even more beneficial.

OPPOSITE Cinnamon seed soap has valuable exfoliating properties, which will boost the condition of your skin – and it smells fabulous too!

dry skin brushing

Before bathing, brush your skin in long sweeping strokes, moving up from the feet and legs, working towards the heart. Long-handled body brushes are available from good health stores and pharmacies. Dry skin brushing not only improves the condition of the skin, but is highly effective at stimulating the removal of toxins by improving lymphatic drainage. Do not brush areas of damaged skin or the sensitive skin on the face and neck.

soaps and talcs

Find handmade soaps that specialize in exfoliation, deep cleansing and purification. Cinnamon seed soap not only has a sweetly aromatic fragrance, but has exfoliating properties, and is an effective massage bar. Lemon grass has toning and antiseptic qualities that are useful for oily skin and acne, and can also help tighten up loose, post-pregnancy or post-diet skin. Seaweed retains moisture and contains beneficial minerals, including iodine. It reduces impurities in fat cells and generally nourishes and improves the skin. To customize your own talcum powder, add 5 drops of essential oil to 1 tbsp of cornflower (cornstarch) and mix with 5 tbsps of unscented talc.

relax
let go
balance

Giving your body and mind a chance to switch off, unwind, and restore its natural balance and harmony is just as important as exercise and a healthy diet. Your home spa environment, filled with soothing fragrances, and with harmonizing oils and lotions to hand, is the perfect haven.

slowing down

Most of us live hectic lives, often juggling too many responsibilities. Use your spa treatments as a time to slow right down and relax. Through relaxation the body's metabolism will readjust and rebalance itself, and you'll feel more in harmony with yourself.

Taking a long bath, enjoying a sensual massage or giving yourself a reflexology treatment are great ways to relax. For added benefit, use your favourite aromatic oils to enhance the mood. Make sure you spend some quiet time every day, a time to just sit and "be", or maybe curl up with a book, or take a walk in nature. Meditation and gentle yoga stretches will quieten the mind and release tension in the body. If you have trouble sleeping, they can be used before bedtime. You can meditate by sitting or lying down; just close your eyes and focus your attention inwards. Focusing on the rise and fall of your breath will help your mind to slow down and clear.

TOP RIGHT Essential oil and water mixes can increase humidity levels and release relaxing aromas.

RIGHT Bach flower remedies such as honeysuckle and vervain can be taken to help you unwind.

OPPOSITE It is important to have some unwinding time every day. Sit or rest quietly and let your mind rest on peaceful thoughts or scenes, or let it empty completely.

simple yoga stretches

Exercise plays an important role in your home spa treatments. Yoga is particularly suitable, as you do not need any special equipment and you can do it indoors at any time of the day. It is also the perfect method for relaxing and letting go, releasing physical tension and mental stress, and restoring body and mind to a state of balance.

child pose

This is a classic loosening up exercise. Sit on your heels and breathe in. Breathe out to bend forward. Place your forehead on the floor, bringing your arms close to your feet. If your chest or bust feels compressed, you may prefer to rest your forehead on a cushion. Breathe into your ribs at the back to expand your breathing for a few moments.

corpse pose

This is a great relaxer – so called because all the muscles relax and your body becomes a dead weight. Lie flat on your back on a firm surface, such as the

TOP Yoga teaches us that we can make a choice to relax whenever and wherever we want.

LEFT The child pose works to loosen up your upper back and shoulders, as well as your knees and ankles.

floor, and cover yourself with a blanket. Let your arms rest slightly away from your sides, palms up, with your legs straight and hip-width apart. If your chin juts up, place a cushion under your head. If your waist arches, place a cushion under your knees. It takes time to find your most relaxing position. Then, feel your whole body sinking into the ground, close your eyes and let your thoughts drift away.

arm and chest stretch

This stretch for the upper body can be done standing or sitting back on your heels. If kneeling, you may find it more comfortable to put a cushion between your heels and buttocks. Hold your body up straight and breathe in. Breathing out, stretch the spine up, bringing your clasped hands overhead, and keeping your arms close to your body, palms up. As you breathe out, bring your arms down and your hands back to your lap. Repeat a few times.

opening chest

Stand with your feet hip-width apart. Breathe in and stretch up through your spine. As you breathe out, bend and stretch to the right, keeping your left shoulder back. Breathe in to return to the upright position and, breathing out, stretch to the left. Repeat three times. Now swing your arms and rotate your upper body from side to side, keeping the spine upright and breathing naturally and vigorously.

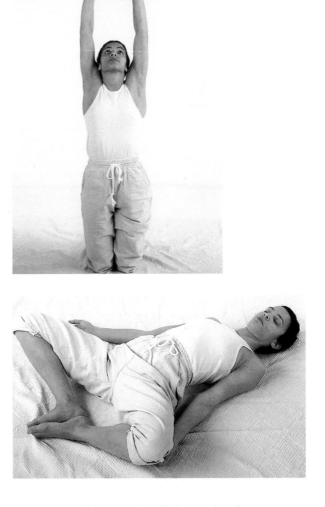

TOP The arm and chest stretch will help you to breathe slowly and deeply, relaxing the heart and reducing stress.

ABOVE The butterfly stretch is a relaxing pose for deep breathing and loosening up the hip joints.

the benefits of massage

Massage is one of the best methods around for encouraging relaxation and is something that you can practise on yourself. It has a calming effect on the nervous system, helping body and mind to let go and unwind, and restoring your system to a state of balance. Gentle, relaxing strokes trigger the release of endorphins, the body's natural painkillers, while a more vigorous rubbing or pressing action will get to work on the underlying muscular structure of the body, stretching tight muscles and easing away any tension knots and stiffness in the joints. As you relax into a peaceful state, your body's self-healing mechanism will kick into action and work more effectively. Before you start, gather together your massage oils, creams or lotions, any candles and essential oils, and a pile of warm, clean towels. Soft relaxing music in the background will also contribute to an atmosphere of peace and calm.

tension relievers

To help you relax and unwind, focus your attention on specific areas of tightness or tension in your body and ease them out with therapeutic massage.

simple self-massage

To relieve headaches caused by mental tiredness, dab a little massage oil on your fingertips and place your fingers and thumbs at the temples. Stretch your fingers on to your forehead and move them firmly from the centre towards the temples and back to the centre. Using the cushions of your middle fingers, make circular movements from the centre of the top of your forehead to the upper temple. Repeat down the forehead, moving from the centre to the temples each time. Finish by pressing your fingers in the temple hollows and make firm circles to move the skin of the temples over the bone beneath.

The muscles in the shoulders and upper back are classic tension points. You can work these yourself, using your hands in a squeezing movement across

TOP Choose a quiet part of the house for your relaxation massage and light scented candles to help you unwind.

LEFT It is instinctive to rub your forehead or temples when you have a headache. Massaging with essential oils is even more effective.

the muscle fibres. Rest one hand over the point of your opposite shoulder. Move your hand firmly along the top of the shoulder to the neck, then return. Feel for any hard tension spots and apply circular pressure with your fingers. Repeat on the opposite shoulder.

reflexology

This exploits the reflexes present in our feet, and uses massage techniques to benefit the whole body. Rest one foot on the knee of your opposite leg and massage the sole with firm circular movements. Notice any painful areas of tension, and use a firm thumb pressure to ease them out. Repeat on the other foot.

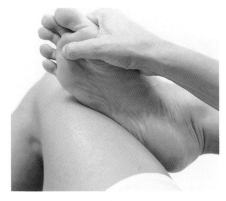

ABOVE Reflexology taps into the natural reflexes of the feet and can bring deep relaxation to the whole body.

TOP RIGHT Tension in the muscles of the back and shoulders can be relieved with firm circular pressure.

RIGHT Sweet marjoram, rosemary and pine essential oils can all be rubbed into the lower back to ease strains.

leisurely bathing

There is nothing like a long leisurely soak in the bathtub to melt away tension. Enjoyed in the evening, a warm bath helps the body to relax and can pave the way for a good night's sleep, free from overactive thoughts and worries. Although you may be tempted, especially in cold weather, to have a steaming hot bath, a 20-minute soak in body-temperature water is far more effective at helping you unwind. Bathing in water that is too hot can cause thread veins and may make you feel unwell. The skin is also better able to release impurities at body temperature and to absorb the healing properties of any herbs and minerals that are added to the bathwater.

To make bathing a real indulgence you can create your own aromatic bath products. A warm bath with a soothing fragrance has to be the highlight of any relaxation session. One of the simplest ways of making your bath special is to add 6–8 drops of essential oil to the water. Bathing enhances the effects of the essential oils, as they are not only absorbed through the skin but their aroma is also inhaled. Lavender, chamomile, clary sage, neroli and rose all have a relaxing soporific effect, lessening anxiety and nervous tension and promoting a good night's sleep. Swish the oil(s) into the bath just before you get in. The oils can be mixed with 15ml/1 tbsp dairy cream, honey or powdered milk before being added to the bath, to help disperse them. If you use powdered milk, make it into a paste before adding to the water.

TOP Add essential oils to your bath water and use a massage roller to soothe tired and aching muscles.

OPPOSITE Gather together any loofahs and soaps you plan to use and keep them within reach of the bath, so that you won't have to disturb your relaxing soak to get them.

after-bath treatments

Bathing is not complete without pampering your body with fragrant dusting powders, and lotions and creams to remoisturize the skin. If you like, you can finish with a delicate touch of cologne or perfume, building up layers of fragrance for a lingering effect.

In ancient Egypt, high-ranking officials would sleep in beds scented with fragrant powders. They believed that as they slept the fragrance was better absorbed by the skin and longer lasting. If you don't want to go to such extremes, a soft dusting of powder over your body after bathing will have a similar effect. To customize your own blend, use a base of unscented talc and add your chosen fragrances. A blend of 3 drops each of lavender, coriander (cilantro), lemon, and geranium essential oils mixed with 175ml/6fl oz/ $^3/_4$ cup of unscented talc creates a soft, subtle perfume.

Water has a drying effect on the skin, particularly if you stay in the bath for too long. To help the skin regain its moisture, make liberal use of body lotions. Both rose and lavender have remarkable properties, helping the skin to regenerate at a cellular level. Rose is also excellent for dry skin and combines well with geranium. Mix 10–15 drops of oil with 175ml/6fl oz/ $^3/_4$ cup of unscented body lotion and pour into a bottle. For a face cream, mix 5 drops of essential oil per 50ml/2fl oz/$^1/_4$ cup unscented cream base.

LEFT If you haven't got time for a full bath, a foot bath is a good second best. Soak your feet for at least 10 minutes.

OPPOSITE Add a blend of your favourite essential oils to unscented creams and lotions for nourishing body care.

complete relaxation

ABOVE If you have a glut of perfumed roses in your garden during summer, you can harvest their petals for home-made preparations with a healing effect.

OPPOSITE Go to bed with a sleep pillow filled with mildly sedative herbs and flowers such as hops, chamomile, rose or jasmine.

The ability to relax and let go completely is probably the most important part of your spa routine. Give yourself permission to switch off and take a little extra time afterwards to get the most out of your relaxing treatments. To jump up and move too quickly into a work or household task would be to undo all your good work.

Burning candles and using incense or aromatic oil-burners will help to create the mood for relaxation. Allow yourself at least 10 minutes just to sit quietly with your eyes closed and your mind switched off, and breathe in the beneficial aromas. The essential oils of sandalwood and frankincense have a soothing and calming effect, slowing down the breathing and helping to release mental tension. Lavender is also very relaxing and soothing.

To help you unwind from the inside out, herbal preparations can be very useful. Herbal remedies that will help after a stressful day include wild oats, licorice and borage. For a calming tea, put 5ml/1 tsp of each of the herbs (avoiding licorice if you have high blood pressure) into a tea pot or cafetière, top up with boiling water and leave to infuse for 10 minutes before straining. Nervous anxiety can be calmed with St John's wort or skullcap in the same way. Try to drink one cup of the tea three times a day for best results. Valerian, hops, lime blossom, passionflowers and lavender all have a sedating effect and can be taken at bedtime to promote a restful healing sleep. Add 25g/1oz of the dried herb (or 50g/2oz fresh) to 475ml/16fl oz/2 cups of boiling water to make an infusion. Strain off the mixture and sweeten with honey to taste.

restore
strengthen
heal

This section is about blitzing those weak spots, the areas that need and deserve special attention beyond daily care. It is about healing treatments, but also about making your body's most vulnerable points stronger and better able to withstand the pressures of everyday life.

ready to regenerate

The human body has an amazing ability to regenerate itself. Every day cells are renewed and the body's natural self-healing mechanism actively works to repair damage and restore balance. A healthy living plan, together with special treatments that restore, strengthen and heal, will help to maintain your body in peak condition.

Sleep is an essential natural healing process, for this is when the majority of the body's repair work takes place. How much sleep we need can vary, but most adults need up to eight hours. Eating a healthy diet will give your body the "four star" fuel it needs to keep it running at its optimum. Go easy on foods that place a strain on the body's resources, such as red meat, refined carbohydrates, saturated fats, sugar, alcohol and caffeine. Wholegrains, fresh fruits and vegetables, oily fish and white meats will all help the body to heal and regenerate. Substitute caffeine drinks with invigorating tonic teas, such as peppermint or lemon verbena. Dry skin conditions can be improved by increasing the amount of essential fatty acids (found in vegetable oils and oily fish) in your diet. Supplements such as vitamin E, zinc and evening primrose oil capsules will help too.

Exercise also has a vital role to play in building up the body's strength. Physical activity improves circulation and promotes the elimination of toxins from the lymphatic system; it also encourages restful sleep. Finally, don't forget to nourish your inner self. Good health comes from within, so take time each day to relax completely, emptying your mind of negative or active thoughts, and restoring yourself to a state of peace and harmony.

TOP Citrus fruits have antiseptic and a host of curative and restorative properties.

ABOVE A few drops of lavender oil on the pillow can help you have a good night's sleep.

OPPOSITE Give yourself time to rest each day to allow the body's cells a chance to regenerate.

healing aches and pains

Complementary therapies can be used as a safe, drug-free alternative for treating many everyday aches and pains. After strenuous activity or overuse, sore and aching muscles can be helped with massage or a relaxing soak in the bath. A useful, all-purpose Bach flower essence is Rescue Remedy, which contains a combination of five flower essences.

It is particularly helpful in first-aid situations and for shock. Homeopathic remedies are useful for treating acute infections (coughs, colds and sore throats, for instance) and also in first aid. Aromatherapy can also be used to treat many problems, including headaches and insomnia, while herbal preparations of echinacea and garlic help to strengthen the immune system.

natural remedies

Complementary therapies such as herbalism, homeopathy and aromatherapy can bring effective relief to common health problems. Deciding which one to choose is a matter of personal preference.

head-clearing inhalations

Aromatic steam inhalations are excellent for clearing blocked sinuses, congestive headaches and for coughs, colds and flu. One of the most effective methods of making an inhalant is to immerse fresh herbs and spices in boiling water. Put a handful of herbs such as eucalyptus leaves, basil, hyssop, juniper foliage, mint, lavender, lemon balm, rosemary, sage and thyme into a bowl. Add spices such as cayenne pepper, cinnamon sticks and juniper berries. Pour in 1 litre/ 1³/₄ pints/4 cups of boiling water. Lean over the bowl, cover your head with a towel, and inhale deeply. If you are prone to thread veins or if you are asthmatic, this treatment is not recommended.

homeopathic treatments

Homeopathic pills are taken internally to stimulate the body's self-healing mechanism. Although they work best by considering the whole person, they can also be used to treat localized symptoms. Mouth ulcers can be helped by *merc. sol.*, hangover headaches by *nux vom.* and sneezy, watery colds by *allium cepa*. Flu is usually helped by *gelsemium*, and a dry, barking cough by *bryonia*. For lacerated cuts and wounds, try *hypericum*, use *cantharis* for cystitis, *arnica* for bruising, and *euphrasia* for conjunctivitis and eye problems generally.

TOP Healing compresses reduce inflammation or congestion and soothe abrasions.

ABOVE A steam inhalation using essential oils or an infusion of herbs is a good treatment for respiratory conditions such as bronchitis.

compresses

A compress is an excellent treatment for areas of pain or injury such as strained muscles, headaches, sore joints, period pains and insect bites. Cool compresses are best where there is inflammation or heat, and warm compresses if there is a pain or dull ache.

To make a compress you need a clean cotton cloth and a bowl of water. If using essential oils, stir 5 drops of the oil into the water and place the cloth on the water to absorb the oils. Or you can make an infusion using 25g/1oz dried herbs or 50g/2oz fresh herbs to 475ml/16fl oz/2 cups boiling water. Squeeze out the excess water and position the cloth on the area to be treated. Secure in place with clear film (plastic wrap).

Lavender oil is the most widely used aromatherapy oil and a useful all-rounder, suitable for headaches, stomach and period pains, insect bites, burns and swellings. Tea tree oil is a powerful antiseptic, antiviral and antifungal, and is useful for treating cuts and grazes, wounds, bites, athlete's foot and cold sores. A marigold infusion is also useful for bites and stings as marigold flowers have antiseptic properties and are an immune system stimulant. Marigold also has an affinity with the female reproductive system and can help to ease cramping period pains. Juniper, chamomile and marjoram are very good for muscular aches and pains resulting from sport or over-exertion.

whole body restore

Targeted action to restore the body to optimum health is the next step towards healing and regeneration. A little pampering never fails to boost well-being!

rejuvenating massage

In ancient Rome, elderly and worn-out slaves were given "percussion" massage to rejuvenate them and increase their market value. The technique involves cupping the hands loosely and making light, hacking strokes over all the major muscle groups to tone and restore the body. Although you can do it yourself, there will be some areas that you can't reach, so call in a sympathetic friend to treat you – after about 15 minutes, you'll feel like a new person. The ideal massage oil to use contains tea tree, a great healer with a fresh, resinous smell and wonderful antiseptic properties. If you are massaging yourself, concentrate on the areas of tension around the neck and shoulders. To get the maximum benefit from your massage, follow it with 10 minutes of quiet relaxation.

bathtime conditioning

Dry skin brushing helps to get rid of flaky, dead skin cells and stimulates the body's rejuvenating processes. Do it before taking a regenerating soak in the

ABOVE Use a daily moisturizer on your neck and shoulders, which are prone to dryness. Products that contain the valuable anti-oxidant vitamin E will help to protect the skin against aging.

RIGHT Dry brushing using long, upward strokes is an excellent way to exfoliate the skin, and can boost the circulation in areas such as the backs of arms and legs.

bathtub, remembering to brush up the body towards the heart. A milk and honey bath oil with rosemary is perfect for your healing bath. Milk has a cleansing and lubricating effect when applied to the skin, while the rosemary essential oil is regenerative and healing. Beat 2 eggs and 45ml/3 tbsp pure rosemary essential oil together, then add 10ml/2 tbsp baby shampoo, 15ml/1 tbsp vodka and 150ml/$^1/_4$ pint/ $^2/_3$ cup milk, and mix thoroughly. Pour into a glass screw-topped bottle. Add a little of the oil under the running bathtaps; keep the rest in the fridge and use within a few days.

customized body care

After bathing, pat your skin dry and make liberal use of moisturizing body lotions and creams to pamper and recondition your skin. The arms and legs, particularly, will benefit hugely from some intensive attention. Two of the best essential oils to make use of for conditioning care are neroli and rose. Neroli, made from delicate orange blossom petals, and rose are widely used in commercially made perfume and skincare products. Both oils have a regenerating effect on the skin's cells, improving the skin's elasticity and alleviating thread veins. Rose is particularly suitable for aging or drying skin, and neroli is useful for treating stretch marks. For a customized treatment, add 10–15 drops of oil to 50ml/2fl oz/$^1/_4$ cup of unscented lotion or cream.

ABOVE Goats milk and almond soap will leave your skin feeling creamy soft and smooth. The protein-rich goat's milk nourishes the skin, while almond oil moisturizes.

hands and nails

ABOVE Well cared for hands and nails are a beauty asset. Add geranium oil to a carrier base and work into the skin.

OPPOSITE TOP For dry, cracked knuckles, try patchouli oil mixed in a carrier oil and applied to the affected area.

OPPOSITE BELOW If you apply neat lavender oil to each cuticle daily with a cotton bud (Q-tip) you should have stronger nails after two or three months.

Our hands are usually among the most visible parts of the body yet it is easy to neglect them. They are under constant attack from the elements, and everyday tasks, such as housework or gardening, all take their toll. Hands are a tell-tale sign of a person's age and state of health: dry or brittle nails, for example, suggest a lack of B vitamins, white flecks on the nails imply a shortage of zinc, and generally weak nails are a sign of a calcium deficiency.

Resolve to protect your hands better in the future: use a good quality moisturizer containing UV filters to protect them from the damaging effects of the sun, and get into the habit of wearing gloves for tasks such as gardening and washing dishes. Try rubbing a little neat lavender oil into the cuticles every night – this will help to strengthen the nails.

You can also give your hands a kick start with regenerating treatments to repair some of the damage and improve their appearance. After removing all traces of nail varnish, soak your fingertips in a bowl of warm olive oil for 10 minutes. Then gently rub 5ml/1 tsp salt into the hands. The abrasive action of the salt removes dead skin cells. Next, trim your nails and file them into shape, sweeping from the outer corner of the nail inwards. Ease the cuticles back with an orange stick or cocktail stick wrapped in cotton wool (a cotton ball). Then buff your nails to smooth away any ridges and give a natural shine.

For a hand massage, mix 2 drops of marjoram essential oil with 15ml/1 tbsp almond oil. Pour a little into your palms to warm up the oil, then gently stroke the length of one hand with the other, from the wrist to the fingertips.

rose hand mask

Masks can be used on the hands to restore the tone and texture of the skin. Bind together 45ml/3 tbsp medium oatmeal with 30ml/2 tbsp rose infusion or distilled rose water and 5ml/1 tsp each of almond oil, lemon juice and glycerine, to form a soft paste. Apply the mask evenly over your hands and relax for 15–20 minutes. Rinse the mask off in warm water – your hands should feel soft and smooth.

rich aromatic hand cream

Moisturize your hands at regular intervals throughout the day, particularly when they have been in water. Creams are more readily absorbed when your hands are warm. The chamomile in this hand cream soothes the skin, geranium has healing, antiseptic properties, and lemon has a whitening effect and can help to reduce unsightly age spots. Blend 10 drops of chamomile essential oil and 5 drops each of geranium and lemon with 120ml/4fl oz of unscented hand cream.

feet first

ABOVE A foot bath restores and revitalizes aching feet and sends messages of well-being throughout the body.

Think of the amount of work our feet have to do – we walk on them daily, often in inappropriate footwear, and yet we give them surprisingly little care and attention. Years of friction between shoes, the ground and the bony areas on the feet will result in patches of leathery skin and the development of corns and calluses. Footcare treatments have an important part to play in your home spa.

herbal foot baths

Foot baths have been used for hundreds of years as a way to restore tired feet. You can make a herbal infusion containing a mixture of peppermint, pine needles, chamomile or rosemary, or add 4 drops of essential oil to a bowl of hot water. An Epsom salts bath is good for aching feet and swollen ankles, while an infusion containing cider vinegar, myrrh or tea tree oil treats fungal conditions, such as athlete's foot. These ingredients help to restore the pH balance of the skin; fungal infections occur when the skin becomes over-alkaline. To treat a cold or chill, use a mustard foot bath made up of 15ml/l tbsp mustard powder to 2.2 litres/4 pints/9 cups of hot water. Sit in a comfortable chair with a good book, or listen to some music, and immerse your feet for 20 minutes.

foot softeners

Always moisturize your feet well after bathing because the skin on the feet is drier than elsewhere on the body. A few drops of peppermint oil added to some baby lotion doubles as an effective moisturizer and is a wonderfully cooling remedy for tired, aching feet. If you have cracked skin around the heels, soak your feet for 10 minutes in warm soapy water, then rub at the heels with a pumice stone. After drying, apply a thick layer of petroleum jelly to your heels and pull on a pair of clean cotton socks before going to bed. When you wake in the morning, your feet will feel beautifully soft.

ABOVE Use a blend of essential oils in a base oil to give yourself a foot massage. It feels fantastic and will energize the reflex points on the soles of your feet.

RIGHT Our feet are often neglected but will respond extremely well to regular care and attention.

hair and face restorers

Some really intensive conditioning for your hair and complexion will complete your all-body-restoring home spa programme.

intensive hair repair

This once-a-month deep-conditioning treatment will benefit the scalp and improve the texture of your hair. Combine 90ml/6 tbsp coconut oil with 4 drops of rosemary and 3 drops each of tea tree and lavender oils. This makes enough for five treatments and will keep well if stored in a dark-coloured glass bottle. Apply the oil sparingly before shampooing. Massage in well, working the oil into any split ends. Then cover your head with a hot towel and sit and relax for 15–20 minutes. Rinse off and shampoo as normal. If your hair is greasy, take care not to overstimulate the scalp as you massage in the oil.

For thinning hair, mix of 10ml/2 tsp wheatgerm oil and 30ml/2 tbsp olive oil with 8 drops rosemary, 6 drops patchouli and 1 drop lavender essential oils.

A simple restorative treatment for dry, brittle hair is to boil 45ml/3 tbsp of ground sesame seeds in a little water for 10 minutes, strain through muslin (cheesecloth) and cool. Massage the oil into the hair and leave for 10 minutes before rinsing thoroughly.

OPPOSITE Natural hair care products make use of rosemary, the classic herb for dark hair (though its high essential oil level makes it a good for dry hair of any colour), and chamomile, which adds shine to fair hair.

LEFT It is important to moisturize your skin after a facial, but let it rest for a few minutes before doing so.

facial care

Finally, it's time to nourish your face. Let the beneficial effects of honey and oatmeal sink deep into the skin. Mix 15ml/1 tbsp runny honey, 1 egg yolk together and stir in enough fine oatmeal to make a soft paste. Smooth on to the skin and relax for 15–20 minutes. A chilled chamomile teabag over each eyelid will tone the skin and refresh the eyes. Rinse off with lukewarm water and pat dry. Cotton wool pads soaked in rose water are alternative eye treatments, reducing puffiness and leaving you feeling refreshed and looking wide awake. Follow with a moisturizer.

Index